To dear &

from

Mrs. Soderstrom

Outline Studies on I John

OUTLINE STUDIES
ON I JOHN

A Previously Unpublished Series

by
R. A. TORREY

ZONDERVAN PUBLISHING HOUSE
Grand Rapids, Michigan

These things have I written unto you that believe on the name of the Son of God; that ye may know that ye have eternal life, and that ye may believe on the name of the Son of God.

I John 5:13

CONTENTS

Outline Studies on I John

I JOHN 1

INTRODUCTION: Some years ago in the church of which I was then pastor I took up the First Epistle of John, attempting to expound everything I found in the epistle. It took many weeks to cover the epistle, but they were times of great blessing. I think that they were weeks of the richest blessing I had ever known in my ministry up to that time. I am not proposing at this time to go so extensively into the epistle as I did then, but to give five messages on the book, one on each chapter.

There is no book in the whole Bible that is more profitable for Christians to study, and especially for young Christians, than the First Epistle of John, for this epistle was written by John, under the inspiration of the Holy Spirit, for the specific purpose of meeting the needs of young Christians. John himself has defined his purpose in writing the book. We find his definition of this purpose in the thirteenth verse of the fifth chapter, "These things have I written unto you, that ye may know that ye have eternal life, even unto you that believe on the name of the son of God." It certainly is of the highest importance that every believer should know that he has eternal life. Not only is it important that we have eternal life, but it is of the highest importance that *we know* that we have it, and John here tells us that this sure knowledge will come to us through the study of this book. While this was the main pur-

11

pose John had in mind in writing this book, he states other subsidiary and important purposes that he had in mind, which we will note as we come to them. Chapter one sets forth Seven Present and Priceless Privileges and Possessions of the Believer in Jesus Christ, and it is from that standpoint we will study the chapter.

I. PRECIOUS AND CERTAIN KNOWLEDGE

The first Priceless Privilege and Possession of the Believer set forth in the chapter is that of *Precious and Certain Knowlledge*. This we find in the first and second verses of the chapter: "That which was from the beginning, that which we have heard, that which we have seen with our eyes, that which we beheld, and our hands handled, concerning the Word of life (and the life was manifested, and we have seen, and bear witness, and declare unto you the life, the eternal life, which was with the Father, and was manifested unto us)." Two things in these verses are to be noted:

1. First, *the certainty of the believer's knowledge.* The knowledge which John here imparts is *certain* knowledge; it is not speculation, but what John actually experienced and therefore knew. Note his words, he says, "That which we have *heard*, that which we have *seen with our eyes*, that which we have *beheld*, [the word translated "beheld" is a strong word, which means not merely seen, but gazed at intently, scrutinized] and [that which] our hands handled [i.e., felt of]." When John spoke of eternal life he was not following cunningly devised fables, he was not following philosophical speculations. He had heard Jesus, in whom the life was, with his own ears. He had seen Jesus, in whom this life was incarnated, with his own eyes. He had not merely seen Him with a passing gaze, he had studied Him intently. Yes, he had felt Him with his own hands. The

knowledge which we believers have today is founded upon the testimony of these careful *eye witnesses*, it is *certain knowledge*.

Christianity is not a religion of speculations, but of carefully observed and well established facts. The believer in Jesus Christ has then a knowledge that is not only incomparably precious but absolutely sure. I am glad I know eternal life, and I am glad my knowledge of it is not built upon the speculations of philosophers or even theologians, but on the unimpeachable testimony of those who heard, saw, gazed at, and handled Him in whom it was incarnate. It is not merely a lovely dream, but solid fact, carefully observed and an accurately recorded fact.

2. The second thing to be noted is, *just what it is the believer knows*. The believer knows *"Eternal Life."* John says, "I declare unto you *the life, the eternal life,* which was with the Father and was manifested [i.e., made visibly manifest] unto us." That eternal life is not something the Christian is left to speculate about. Eternal life has been manifested, has been made visibly apparent. It was manifested in the person of Jesus Christ. Jesus Christ was a living embodiment of eternal life. Does someone say, "I would like to know what eternal life is, I would like to see it"? Well then, look at Jesus Christ. Just what "eternal life" is you will see in Him. The eternal life that was with the Father from all eternity has been manifested here on earth in time, it was manifested in Jesus Christ, and you and I may know it, we may know just what it is; we know just what it is by looking at Him, and in Him *we see* eternal life, we see the manifested life of God.

Could there by any possibility be any more precious knowledge than the knowledge of eternal life? To know philosophy may be good, to know real science may be even better than to know philosophy, but to know either philosophy or science or both together or anything else, is nothing in comparison with knowing eternal life, and it is the privilege of every believer in Jesus Christ to know this eternal life which through all eternity was with the Father and in the incarnation of Jesus Christ was manifested to us here on earth and observed by those who heard it, saw it, gazed at it and felt it.

II. GLORIOUS FELLOWSHIP

The second Priceless Privilege of the Believer that John speaks of in this chapter is the believer's Glorious Fellowship. John says in the third verse, "That which we have seen and heard declare we unto you also, that ye also may have fellowship with us: Yea, and *our fellowship is with the Father, and with his Son Jesus Christ.*" Is not that glorious fellowship? Fellowship *with God the Father and with Jesus Christ His Son?* The word translated "fellowship" means "companionship," or "comradeship," or "intimacy," it means "partnership." This is the Priceless Privilege and Possession, the *Present* Privilege and Possession of the believer in Jesus Christ, the *companionship* of God the Father and Jesus Christ the Son, the *comradeship* of God the Father and Jesus Christ the Son, the *intimate friendship* of God the Father and Jesus Christ the Son, and more than that, *partnership* with God the Father and Jesus Christ the Son.

Sometimes when we hear of some great one of this earth we think, "Oh, if I could only have fellowship with that man, if I could only have intimate acquaintance and frequent communion with him." But here is something infinitely better than fellowship and intimate acquaintance with any man or woman who ever lived on this earth, no matter how wise and great they may be, fellowship with God the Father and Jesus Christ the Son, and this fellowship is open to all of us.

When we accept Jesus Christ as our personal Saviour God takes us into partnership with Himself. He makes us partners with Himself in His work and also in all that He possesses. We become "heirs of God and joint heirs with Jesus Christ" (Romans 8:17). There are many who hesitate to come to Christ through fear of losing dear and valued earthly friends, but what are the friendships we lose by coming to Jesus Christ compared with the friends we gain? "Our fellowship is with the Father and with his Son Jesus Christ." What matters it if we lose every friend on earth if we enter into fellowship, communion, comradeship, intimate friendship and partnership with God the Father and Jesus Christ the Son?

But just how do we enter into this glorious fellowship? John tells us: "That which we have seen and heard *declare we* unto you, *that ye also may have fellowship with us:* yea, and our fellowship is with the Father, and with his Son Jesus Christ." We enter into this fellowship with the Father and the Son through the knowledge of the written word, through meditation upon what John and the other apostles have declared unto us concerning Jesus Christ. Here is one point where Bible study pays, pays infinitely beyond any other study, because the study of what the apostles have declared about Jesus Christ brings us into fellowship with the apostles themselves, and therefore into fellowship with God the Father and with Jesus Christ the Son. Why is it that most of us have so little fellowship with God the Father and Jesus Christ His Son, so little intimate comradeship and communion?

III. FULLNESS OF JOY

The third Priceless Present Possession of the Believer is Fullness of Joy. This comes out in the fourth verse: "These things we write that your joy may be full." The English Revised Version says "fulfilled." If the revisers had turned the word "fulfilled" around they would have had the exact English equivalent of what John wrote in Greek, *"filled full."* So then we are told here that it is the believer's privilege to have his joy "filled full." Fullness of joy, joy filled up to the very brim, is the present privilege of every believer in Jesus Christ. The world knows joy, but it knows no fullness of joy, its cup is never full, it is never satisfying, but the Christian can say, "My cup runneth over" (Psalm 23:5). This fullness of joy comes through what is written, through the Word of God, "these things we *write* . . ." (cf. Jeremiah 15:16). It comes also from knowing eternal life and from fellowship with God the Father and Jesus Christ the Son. There is no greater earthly joy than the joy of good companionship, but there is no earthly companionship like the companionship of God the Father and Jesus Christ His Son. How earth's highest joys fade when we enter into the joy of fellowship with God the Father and Jesus Christ His Son.

The Revised Version of this verse reads somewhat differently. Instead of reading, "These things write we unto you, that your joy may be full," it changes the word "your" to *"our"* and reads, "These things we write, that our joy may be fulfilled." If we take the rendering of the Revised Version, for which the manuscript evidence is very strong, we get an additional thought, and that is that fullness of joy is found in communicating to others the eternal life and fellowship with God the Father and Jesus Christ the Son which we ourselves have found. Whether this is the thought that John intended to convey or not, it certainly is a true thought. It is the one who gives out to others what God gives to him who finds fullness of joy. It is joyous to find eternal life for ourselves, it is even more joyous to lead others into eternal life. I know of no greater joy, and I doubt if there is any greater joy this side of heaven, than that of leading someone else to know Jesus Christ and thereby to know eternal life and to know the companionship of the Father and of His Son. There are many professing Christians today who do not have fullness of joy, and the reason why they do not have the fullness of joy is because they are content with being saved themselves and they do not go out to save others. Let these words of John sink into our hearts: "These things we write that our joy may be fulfilled," i.e., that our joy may be made full by bringing others into the joy that we ourselves have found.

IV. A WONDERFUL MESSAGE

The fourth Precious and Present Possession of the Believer is *a Wonderful Message*. This message is presented in verse 5, "This then is the message which we have heard from him [i.e., from God] and announce unto you, that *God is light, and in him is no darkness at all*." That message is of incalculable value. Stop a moment and ponder it. "God is light and in him is no darkness at all." Light is a marvelously expressive figure of *holiness, truth,* and *love*. To say that God is light is to say that God is perfect holiness, perfect truth, perfect love. And furthermore, "in him is no darkness at all." There is not one smallest spot of moral imperfection in God. There is not one slightest trace of falsehood in God. There is not one minutest speck of error in God. There is not one faintest shadow of selfishness in God, "He is light and *in him is no darkness at all."* This is a wonderful message, a glorious message.

Have you ever stopped to think what it would mean if the omnipresent Creator and Ruler of this universe were a wicked person and the world were tuned to wickedness? One night this thought came to me, suppose that God, instead of being light and in Him no darkness at all, had been a wicked being. My brain fairly staggered as I contemplated this possibility and its consequences. The whole universe in that case would be an eternal hell. But thank God it is not so, "God is light and in him is no darkness at all," not one trace of moral or intellectual imperfection in Him, infinite wisdom, infinite holiness, infinite love. My whole being swelled with praise as that glad and glorious truth took possession of me and I turned away from the other frightful thought.

This wonderful message that "God is light and in him is no darkness at all" has important implications. If "God is light" and there is "no darkness at all" in Him, then of necessity God's guidance must always be clear guidance. There are many persons who wish to obey God and who feel impulses to do various things which they think may be the Divine leading, but they are not at all sure and so they hesitate to follow these leadings. Then they are tormented with the thought that perhaps they have disobeyed God in not following these uncertain promptings and leadings.

Sometimes in this way men and women are plunged into the deepest distress of mind for fear that they have disobeyed God, but this distress of mind is entirely unnecessary, for "God is light and in him is no darkness at all." Therefore, if I am God's child and really wish to know and do His will I have a right to expect that He will make His will as clear as day to me.

Any dark, confused leadings are not of Him. Provided my will is surrendered absolutely to Him, His guidance will be as clear as day. He is light, in Him is no darkness at all. If some leading comes to me that I think may be of Him, but regarding which I am not certain, I have a right to say, "Father, Thou art light, and in Thee is no darkness at all. Now I wish to do Thy will. If this prompting is of Thee, if this be Thy will, make it as clear as day and I will do it." And God will make it clear as day, if we really desire to know and do His will; for "God is light and in him is no darkness at all." And if we will live in the power of this truth it will deliver us from our anxieties and worries lest some confused leading may be of Him and lest we may have disobeyed and displeased Him.

There is another inference from this truth that "God is light and in him is no darkness at all," which John himself draws right here in the context, in verse 6, "If we say that we have fellowship with him, and walk in darkness, we lie, and do not the truth." Two cannot walk together unless they be agreed, therefore if God is light there can be no fellowship with Him on our part if we walk in darkness. To walk in darkness is to walk in sin, to walk in disobedience to the known will of God, to walk in error and hate. Any man who is doing that which he knows to be contrary to the will of God, that which he knows to be displeasing to God, is walking in darkness. Any man who is holding on to that which he knows in the depths of his soul to be error, is walking in darkness. Any man who harbors hate in his heart is walking in darkness (I John 2:9), and anyone who in any of these ways is walking in darkness cannot have fellowship with God, and if he says that he has he lies and does not the truth.

Now there are many who are walking in darkness and yet

who profess to have fellowship with God. Everyone who makes
such a profession is a liar. John makes this clear in the sixth
verse. "If we say that we have fellowship with him, and walk
in darkness, we lie, and do not the truth." No matter what
ecstatic experiences you may have, or fancy that you have, if
you are walking in darkness you have no fellowship with God.
So I put to each one of you the question, Are you walking
in the light? Are you leading a life of absolute surrender to the
will of God? Are you studying the Word of God daily that
you may find out what the will of God is? Have you given up
everything which in your deepest and best moments you know
to be error? Have you by the power of God's Holy Spirit ban-
ished every trace of bitterness and hate toward anyone from your
heart? Are you walking in the light?

V. A Holy Walk

The fifth Present and Priceless Privilege and Possession
of the Believer in Jesus Christ is *a Holy Walk*. This we find
in verse 7, "But if we walk in the light, as he is in the light,
we have fellowship one with another, and the blood of Jesus
Christ his Son cleanseth us from all sin." Here we are plainly
told that *it is our privilege to walk in the light,* to walk in the
knowledge of and obedience to the truth, to walk in holiness,
and to walk in love, love to God and our fellowman. Jesus
is Himself the light, and the one who follows Him shall not
walk in darkness, but shall have the light of life (John 8:12).
Walking in the light is indeed a priceless privilege. Should
someone ask you, "Where are you walking?" it is your privilege to triumphantly answer, "I am walking in the light."

VI. CLEANSING FROM ALL SIN

The sixth Present and Priceless Privilege and Possession of the Believer is found in this same seventh verse, and that is *Cleansing from all Sin*. As John puts it, "If we walk in the light, as he is in the light, we have fellowship one with another, and *the blood of Jesus Christ his Son cleanseth us from all sin.*" The cleansing spoken of in this verse is cleansing from the guilt of sin. Whenever in the Bible cleansing is spoken of in connection with the blood, it always has reference to the removal of guilt, i.e., to pardon, and not to removal of the actual presence of sin. The removal of the presence of sin comes in verse 9 and is not referred to here. If I walk in the light, the blood of Jesus Christ removes from me all my guilt, every trace of guilt for all the sins I have ever committed. If I am walking in the light, I am in God's sight as if I had never committed sin in all my life. Jesus Christ by the shedding of His blood made complete atonement for my sin, He took my place, and if I am walking in the light, I have stepped into His place, the place of perfect acceptance before God. There is not one trace of sin upon me. What a priceless possession this is, to have all my sins washed away and to be made white as snow.

Your life may have been full of sin, you may have committed almost every vile deed that one can imagine, your life may be as black as midnight; but, if today you accept Jesus Christ as your Saviour and Lord and thus begin to walk in the light, all that sin is instantly washed away and kept washed away, *all* of it, by the cleansing blood of Jesus Christ. And this is not a future cleansing, but a present cleansing. There are some who hope to have their sins cleansed some day, perhaps after years of struggle, perhaps in some purgatory after death. Thank God that is not the doctrine of the Bible. The doctrine of the

Bible is that of this verse, "If we walk in the light, as he is in the light, we have fellowship one with another, and the blood of Jesus Christ his Son *cleanseth* [i.e., cleanses right now] us from *all* sin." Not one trace of sin is left.

Some seek cleansing by denying their sin, by trying to make out they have no sin to cleanse. No cleansing can be found in that way. Rather, as John tells us in the next verse, "If we say that we have no sin we deceive ourselves, and the truth is not in us." This shows the utter folly of the Christian Science philosophy that seeks to deliver from sin by denying sin, by calling it "illusion" or "mortal thought." But if instead of trying to deny our sin, to cover our sin, we uncover it to God, if we confess it fully to God, He covers it up, or as the next verse puts it, "If we confess our sins, he is faithful and righteous to forgive us our sins, and to cleanse us from all unrighteousness." God's faithfulness and God's righteousness are pledged to the forgiveness of all my sins when I confess them to Him. For me to doubt that my sin is forgiven, if I am a believer in Jesus Christ and have confessed my sin to God, is for me to make God a liar, it is for me to question His faithfulness to His promise and to question His righteousness.

VII. CLEANSING FROM ALL UNRIGHTEOUSNESS

There is one more Priceless Privilege and Possession of the Believer set forth in this chapter. It is found in the verse which I have just quoted: "If we confess our sins, he is faithful and righteous to forgive us our sins, and to cleanse us from all unrighteousness." This seventh privilege is *Cleansing From All Unrighteousness*. Not only is it our present privilege to be cleansed from all the guilt of our sin by the blood, it is also our privilege to be cleansed from all unrighteousness in our life; and when we confess the sins already committed, God not only forgives them, but furthermore delivers us from the power of sin and cleanses us from all unrighteousness in our daily living. It is the believer's blessed present privilege to lead by grace a righteous life, i.e., a life conformed to the will of God as He reveals it to us in His Word. This is not possible for us in our own strength, but it is possible for us by God's grace through the daily working of His Holy Spirit, or, as Paul puts it in Romans 8:3, 4, "For what the law could not do, in that it was weak through the flesh, God, sending his own Son in the likeness of sinful flesh, and as an offering for sin, condemned sin in the flesh: that the ordinance of the law might be fulfilled in us who walk not after the flesh, but after the Spirit." In other words, when we have accepted Jesus Christ as our personal Saviour and made a full surrender to Him, and made a definite confession of the sins that come into our life, and look to God by His grace ministered by the Holy Spirit to do in us the things we cannot do in our own strength, God daily, by the power of His Holy Spirit, gives us victory over our temptations, over our besetting sins, and cleanses us from all unrighteousness in our daily conduct.

CONCLUSION: Here then are the Seven Priceless and Present Privileges and Possessions of the Believer in Jesus Christ as set forth in this chapter: Precious and Certain Knowledge, Glorious Fellowship, (i.e., fellowship with the Father and with His Son Jesus Christ), Fullness of Joy, A Wonderful Message, A Holy Walk, Cleansing From All the Guilt of Sin, Cleansing From All Unrighteousness. Have you claimed these privileges for yourself? Will you claim them today? Are you walking in the full enjoyment of them?

I JOHN 2

SEVEN COMFORTING VIEWS OF JESUS

INTRODUCTION: In our study of I John 1 we considered Seven Present Priceless Privileges and Possessions of the Believer. In the chapter before us now we have presented to us Seven Comforting Views of Jesus, and we will study the chapter from that standpoint:

I. JESUS AS OUR ADVOCATE WITH THE FATHER

The first view of Jesus that the chapter gives us is found in the first verse: "If any man sin, we have an Advocate with the Father, Jesus Christ the righteous."

Here we see our Lord Jesus as our Advocate with the Father.

Jesus always represents all believers in Himself before the throne of God; He pleads our case for us every time we fail and fall into sin. We do not need to sin, God has made abundant provision to keep us from sinning. This is revealed in the first part of this same verse: "My little children, these things write I unto you, that [more exactly, *in order that*] ye may not sin." These words tell us plainly that we do not need to sin, that God has provided by His written Word to keep us from sinning. If we hide God's Word in our hearts as we should it will keep us from sinning. Sin is unnecessary (Psalm 119:11). But suppose, though sin is unnecessary, that we do sin, what then? Is our case hopeless? It is not. In that case, as this verse tells us, we have One to plead our cause before God, and that One is "Jesus Christ, the Righteous [One]" and He Himself has told us in John 11:42 that the Father always hears Him.

Oh, how abundant is the provision that God has made for our salvation and our security in our Lord Jesus Christ, provision fully made that we need not sin, and provision also made in case we do sin. The believer is secure in any event. We have an illustration of this security of the believer through the advocacy of our Lord Jesus Christ in the case of Peter. Satan, as we are told in Luke 22:31, 32, prayed that he might get Simon Peter in his sieve and he did get him, gave him a terrible shaking up, but our Lord said, "Simon, Simon, behold, Satan asked to have you, that he might sift you as wheat: but I made supplication for thee that thy faith fail not," and this supplication of our Advocate made Simon perfectly secure even though he was in Satan's sieve; so our Lord went on to say, being perfectly sure that Simon after his sifting and his sin would return again back to Him and away from sin, "And do thou, when once thou hast turned again, establish thy brethren." Simon was perfectly safe even while in Satan's sieve because Jesus was praying for him, and just so when Satan assaults us, we are perfectly safe.

In the first place, we need not sin, and in the second place even if we do sin, if we are believers in Jesus Christ, then He acts as our Advocate and secures our forgiveness and our repentance. Satan assaults us from two different directions: he comes to us and tells us it is utterly futile to try to live without sinning, that all men sin, and so we must sin, too, and that we might as well sin, and it will not be of much consequence if we do, that God expects no better of us. Then when we do sin he attacks us from the other side and says: "Aha, you are lost; you have sinned; there is no hope for you now, you have sinned willfully after you have received a knowledge of the truth, and there remaineth no more sacrifice for sin, and you might just as well plunge deeply into sin now, you are lost anyhow." The verse which we are studying meets both these lines of Satan's assault; it says to us first of all: "You do not need to sin, sufficient grace is provided in Jesus Christ, no matter how weak you are, to keep you from sinning." But if we do sin after all, this verse meets Satan's other lie and says: "There is hope for you even yet, 'If any man sin, we have an advocate with the Father, Jesus Christ the righteous.'" This is a most comforting view of our Lord Jesus. I am glad to know I do not need to sin, but I am also glad to know that even if I do sin Jesus Christ the Righteous One, will take my case up in the very highest court from which there is no appeal, and carry it through and God will acquit me. Is there some believer in Jesus Christ who has sinned and is in despair? Listen to these words again: "If any man sin, we have an Advocate with the Father, Jesus Christ the righteous [one]."

But before we leave this view of Jesus Christ, let us note carefully just who it is that has an Advocate with the Father. It does not say that all men have an advocate with the Father, Jesus Christ the Righteous (One), it says *we* have an Advocate with the Father," and this "we," we are clearly told, means the believer in Jesus Christ. This is evident from the fifth chapter and the thirteenth verse of the book, where we read, "These things have I written unto you. . . . *that believe on the name of the Son of God.*" The same truth is found in John 17:9 where our Lord Jesus says in speaking to the Father, "I pray *for them:* I pray not for the world, but for those whom thou hast given me; for they are thine." Anyone who does not believe on the Lord Jesus Christ, i.e., anyone who has not received the Lord Jesus

Christ as his personal Saviour and surrendered to Him as his Lord, has no Advocate with the Father. Oh, what a blessed thing it is to be a believer in Jesus Christ and to have this Advocate with the Father always at His right hand, this Advocate whom the Father always hears and who is "able to save to the uttermost them that come unto God through Him, seeing that He ever liveth to make intercession for them" (Hebrews 7:25).

II. JESUS AS A PROPITIATION

The second comforting view which this chapter gives us of Jesus is found in the second verse: "And he is *the propitiation for our sins;* and not for ours only but also for the whole world." Here we see Jesus Christ as a "propitiation for our sins." The word translated "propitiation" means "a means of appeasing" and the thought is that Jesus is a propitiation for our sins by His atoning death, that because of His atoning death on the cross God's wrath at us as sinners is fully appeased. God is a holy God and therefore hates sin. God's holy wrath at sin must strike somewhere, it must either strike on us the sinners, or somewhere else.

It has struck on Jesus Christ, as Isaiah puts it in Isaiah 53:6, "All we like sheep have gone astray; we have turned every one to his own way; and Jehovah hath laid on him the iniquity of us all." The word here translated "laid" means literally "made to strike," and the thought clearly is that Jehovah hath made to strike on our Lord Jesus the iniquity of us all, that Jesus has borne God's wrath at our sin in our place. That indeed is a most wonderfully comforting view of Jesus. I have not one particle of dread of God's wrath at my sin, not one particle. Why not? Because God's wrath at my sin has been satisfied; it is fully *appeased.* God now looks upon me with perfect favor because His wrath at my sin has been appeased by the shed blood of Jesus Christ. Is not that glorious?

Now note carefully for whose sin it is that Jesus is a propitiation. The verse tells us plainly that "He is the propitiation for *our* sins," i.e., for the sins of the believer. If you are united to Jesus by a living faith all your sins, past, present, and future have been settled forever.

> Jesus paid my debt,
> All the debt I owe,
> Sin had left a crimson stain,
> He washed it white as snow.

When? When He died on the Cross.

There is, however, a sense in which Jesus is a propitiation for the whole world. He is not a propitiation for *the sins* of the whole world, but He is a propitiation for the whole world. The Authorized Version of our verse says: "He is the propitiation for the sins of the whole world," but you will notice that the words *"the sins of"* are printed in italics, which indicates that they are not in the original. As they are not found in the original they should not be found in the translation, and so the Revised Version properly omits these words and reads, "He is the propitiation for our sins; and not for ours only, but also for the whole world," thus clearly indicating that the propitiation that Christ made stands in a different relation to the believer's sins from what it does to the sins of others. Jesus is not a propitiation for the world in the sense that He is for the believer. "He is a propitiation for our sins," not for the sins of the world, but He is a propitiation for the world, i.e., the death of Jesus Christ has provided for the whole world, and for every man, woman and child in it, a basis upon which God deals in mercy with the whole world. If it were not for the atoning death of Jesus Christ

God must have destroyed man as soon as sin came into human life, but on the ground of Christ's death God has dealt with man in mercy through all the centuries.

But someone may ask, "How could God deal in mercy on the ground of Christ's death before Christ died?" The answer to this question is given in Revelation 13:8, where we are told that the Lord Jesus is from the foundation of the world "the Lamb that hath been slain." In God's thought the death of Jesus Christ was an eternal fact, it was provided before sin ever entered, and on the ground of this death which God had provided and which was historically to take place later, all God's dealings in mercy with man since sin entered have been based. God deals with the vilest infidel on the ground of the very death he scoffs at. The propitiatory death of Christ avails for everyone; it secures mercy for every child of Adam, but it fully avails only for those who accept it. So we see that Jesus is indeed "the Saviour of all men," as Paul says in I Timothy 4:10, but He is also, as Paul says in the same verse, the Saviour "SPECIALLY of them that believe."

III. JESUS AS AN ABIDING PLACE, OR AS OUR LIFE

The third comforting view of Jesus with which this chapter presents us we see in verse 6: "He that saith he abideth in him ought himself also to walk even as he walked." Here we see Jesus as our "Abiding Place," or as our Life. It is our privilege to abide, or live in Jesus Christ, to live and move and have our being in Him; to draw our very life from Him. We have similar words in John 15, where Jesus Himself teaches us that we may and ought to abide in Him, just as the living, fruit-bearing branch abides in the vine. This, too, is a most comforting view of Jesus, just to think that He not only pleads our cause when we sin, and is not only a propitiation for our sins, but that He imparts His very life unto us, that He is "our life" (cf. Colossians 3:4), that I can live in Him every day and every hour, and draw all my life from Him. But what will be the result if I do thus live in Him and draw my life from Him? I will live as He lived, "he that saith he abideth in him ought himself also to walk even as he walked." Here is found the secret of doing as Jesus would do, the secret of following in His steps: *abide in Him,* renounce your own life and your own strength and take His life and His strength; look to Him every day and hour, for His life to flow into you. It is your privilege and mine to do this.

IV. Jesus As the Anointer

The fourth comforting view of Jesus is found twice in this chapter, in verses 20 and 27: "And ye have an anointing from the holy one. . . . and as for you, the anointing which ye received of [from] him abideth in you, and ye need not that any one teach you; but as his anointing teacheth you concerning all things, and is true, and is no lie, and even as it taught you, ye abide in him." *Here we see Jesus as the Anointer.* The Holy One of verse 20 from whom we receive the anointing is Jesus, and the anointing that we receive from Him is the Holy Spirit. This is a most precious view of our Lord Jesus, Jesus pouring out the oil of the Holy Spirit upon our heads. Never forget that it is He who does it.

This is also evident from Acts 2:33, "Therefore being by the right hand of God exalted, and having received of the Father the promise of the Holy Ghost, he hath poured forth this, which ye see and hear." If you wish to be anointed with the Holy Spirit the Lord Jesus is the One to whom to go for the anointing. Do you know Him as the Anointer, the Anointer with the Holy Ghost? There is no other oil so soft and grateful and fragrant as that. In Hebrews 1:9, this oil is called "the oil of gladness." David said of Jehovah, his Divine Shepherd and Host, "Thou anointest my head with oil." Can you say that of Jesus? "Thou anointest my head with oil."

And what is the result when He does thus anoint us with the Holy Ghost? Verse 27 answers the question: "The anointing which ye received of him abideth in you, and ye need not that any one teach you." When Jesus is taken as your Anointer, when He anoints you with His Holy Spirit, you need no human teacher, the anointing you have received, the Holy Spirit, teaches you all things. This is the same promise that the Lord Jesus made to His disciples in John 14:26: "But the Comforter, even the Holy Spirit, whom the Father shall send in my name, he will teach you all things, and bring to your remembrance all that I said unto you," and repeated in John 16:13, 14: "Howbeit when he, the Spirit of truth is come, he shall guide you into all truth: for he shall not speak from himself, but what things soever he shall hear, these shall he speak: and he shall declare unto you the things that are to come. He shall glorify me: for he shall take of mine, and declare it unto you." John here applies these wonderful promises to all believers. It is every believer's privilege, even the humblest and most underrated believer's privilege, to have the Holy Spirit for his teacher and thus to be independent of human teachers. Is it not a wonderful privilege to have the Holy Spirit for our Teacher? It makes the Bible a new Book; it makes Jesus Himself a new Person. Of course, this does not mean for one moment that we shall learn nothing from others. If John had meant that, he would not have taken the trouble to write this epistle to instruct others. But it does mean that the humblest believer in Jesus Christ is independent of human teachers, he does not need to go to either priest or theological professor — he needs to call no man master, for he can have the Holy Spirit Himself for his teacher. In the Middle Ages (and even now in Roman Catholic lands) the priests sought to take the Bible away from the common people. They said, "You cannot understand the Bible, you must come to us to interpret it for you." And just so now, many who parade as "scholarly critics" are trying to take the Bible away from the common people. They are saying, "You cannot understand the Bible. You haven't taken university courses, you must come to us to interpret the Bible for you. You think it means what it says. Not at all, that is a mistake. You must come to us and let us not only translate Hebrew and Greek words into corresponding English words, but let us trans-late the false and outgrown conclusions of Christ and the apos-tles into our modern and correct conclusions." "No, no, no!" says God. "If you have Jesus as your Teacher, you need not that any man (priest, pope or theological professor) teach you. The Holy Spirit will teach you."

The question is often asked of me: "What shall common ordinary believers do when great theologians and honored Bi-ble teachers so differ among themselves? How shall we ordinary Christians know the truth?" This verse contains the answer to the question: Go directly to the Lord Jesus as your Anointer with the Holy Spirit, and let Him anoint you with the Holy Spirit that you may have Him for your Teacher, and then you can decide for yourself what the truth is as well as the most learned theologian can decide — far better than he can de-cide unless he is a Spirit-filled man.

V. JESUS AS THE CHRIST AND THE SON OF GOD

The fifth comforting view of Jesus presented to us in this chapter we find in verses 22 and 23: "Who is the liar but he that denieth that Jesus is the Christ? This is the antichrist, even he that denieth the Father and the Son. Whosoever denieth the Son the same hath not the Father; he that confesseth the Son hath the Father also." Here we see *our Lord Jesus as the Christ and the Son of God.* This is also a comforting view of Jesus; indeed it is a view that gives comfort to all the other views. If Jesus were not the Son of God His advocacy would be of little value, and His propitiation would be of no avail. If he were not Divine we could not draw life from Him, and it would be of no use to abide in Him. If He were not Divine He could not anoint us with the Holy Spirit, and it is because He is the Christ (that is, the anointed of God) that He can in turn anoint us with the Holy Spirit (cf. Acts 2:33). But He is the Christ and He is the Son of God. Men deny it in these days, they deny it most vociferously, but they lie when they deny it. How emphatically John brings that out in these verses: "Who is *the* liar," he thunders, "but he that denieth that Jesus is the Christ? *This* is the antichrist, even he that denieth the Father and the Son." *"The* liar," the supreme liar, the liar of liars, is the one who denies the Messiahship and the Deity of Jesus Christ. There are those who tell us that Jesus is not the "Christ" of Gentile believers, that He is not the "Christ" of the Jews, but the "Lord" of believers. But just look at the epistles written to the Gentile churches. Look, for example, at the epistle to the Ephesians, and see how He is called "Christ" even in that epistle.

Look at Jesus then and see in Him God's Anointed, your rightful King, yes, your Anointed Prophet, Priest and King. See in Him the Son of God, your Lord and Master. Bow down and worship Him and then give yourself up wholeheartedly to His service.

VI. JESUS AS THE GREAT PROMISER

The sixth comforting view of Jesus given us in this chapter we see in verse 25, "And this is the promise which he promised us, even the life eternal." *Here we see Jesus as the Great Promiser.* He promises us eternal life. In the original this is very emphatic. Literally translated it would read: "This is the promise which he promised to us, the life, the eternal." In chapter one, verse two, the Revised translates exactly the same Greek words, "the life, the eternal life," and they should have been consistent with themselves and so translated it here.

What a wonderful promise that is. No promise of earth can compare with that. We are so familiar with the phrase "life eternal," that we oftentimes miss its wondrous significance. "Eternal life!" Think of it, a life that is absolutely endless in its duration, a life that is absolutely perfect in its quality, yes, absolutely Divine in its quality. Some twenty years ago I began thinking one day of how many more years I had to live and work. As I thought I said to myself, "Not many on earth, possibly thirty, not more probably." Twenty of those thirty years have already passed. Then the thought came to me, "Why man, you have a whole eternity to live." Oh, praise God! I don't feel old, I am very young — in the scale of eternity. "This is the promise which he promised us, even the life eternal." And He will keep His promise. I would not give up that promise for the wealth of all the Rockefellers and Morgans and Carnegies, and all the rest of the multi-millionaires combined. And that life is not only endless in duration, but absolutely perfect and absolutely Divine in its quality (see chapter 1:2). Is not this a wonderfully comforting view of Christ?

VII. Jesus As the Coming One

There is one more comforting view of Jesus, one of the most comforting of all, given us in this chapter. We find it in verse 28: "And now, my little children, abide in him; that, if he shall be manifested, we may have boldness, and not be ashamed before him *at his coming." Here our Lord Jesus is presented to us as the Coming One.* This is one of the most comforting views of Jesus in the whole chapter, or in the whole Bible. John does not go into the details about it until we get into the next chapter. Jesus came once, and I thank God that He did, for by His coming and His atoning death resulting from that coming, I obtained pardon and eternal life. But I thank God He is also coming again to perfect that work which He has begun. If you will study the first epistle of John carefully you will find that almost everything in the epistle is built upon and grows out of the words which our Lord Jesus spoke on His last night on earth as recorded in the thirteenth through the sixteenth chapters of the gospel of John. The view of Jesus given us here is built upon those sweet words in John 14:3, "And if I go and prepare a place for you, I will come again, and will receive you unto myself; that where I am, there ye may be also." These words were spoken for the comfort of believers during the absence of their Lord. Just before uttering them Jesus said, "Let not your heart be troubled," and then He goes on to give them this promise to keep their hearts from being troubled. And this is the great central truth to banish all trouble, all tumult, all anxiety from the heart, "I will come again." We live in tumultuous times, uncertain and anxious times, but this thought keeps my heart calm, no matter how disturbing the news in the papers may seem, for Jesus is coming again. Yes, Jesus is coming again. That is the best news I know. God grant that coming may be soon. But perhaps some of you will be ashamed before Him at His coming, instead of being delighted with His coming. The verse tells us how not to be ashamed but on the contrary, how to have boldness at His coming. Let us read it again: "And now, my little children, abide in him; that, if he shall be manifested, we may have boldness, and not be ashamed before him at his coming."

CONCLUSION: In this chapter, then, we have seven comforting views of Jesus: Jesus our Advocate, Jesus our Propitiation, Jesus our Life, Jesus the Anointer with the Holy Ghost, Jesus the Christ and the Son of God, Jesus the Great Promiser, and Jesus the Coming One. Do you know Him as your Advocate? Do you know Him as your Propitiation? Do you know Him as your Life? Do you know Him as the Anointer with the Holy Ghost? Do you know Him as the Christ the Son of God? Do you know Him as the Great Promiser? Do you know Him as the Coming One? Are you living in the power of these seven great views of Jesus? If you do thus know Him, how can you keep from going out and telling others about Him as you know Him? Perhaps you are not even a Christian. Then I beseech you to become one right now. Accept Jesus as your Propitiation right now; trust Him as your Advocate right now; receive Him as your Life right now; know Him as your Anointer right now; worship Him as your Christ right now; believe Him as your Promiser right now; begin right now to look for Him as your Coming Saviour.

I JOHN 3

A Glad New Year's Message — Seven Great Facts About Believers in Jesus Christ

INTRODUCTION: In our study of I John 1 we saw Seven Present and Priceless Privileges and Possessions of the Believer in Jesus Christ. In the second chapter we found Seven Comforting Views of Jesus. In the third chapter, which we study now, we find Seven Great Facts About Believers in Jesus Christ.

I. Believers in Jesus Christ Are *NOW* Children of God

The first great fact about believers we find in verses 1 and 2: "Behold what manner of love the Father hath bestowed upon us, that we should be called children of God; and such we are. For this cause the world knoweth us not, because it knew him not. (2) Beloved, now are we the children of God, and it is not yet made manifest what we shall be. We know that, if he shall be manifested, we shall be like him; for we shall see him even as he is." The great fact about believers here set forth is that we are *now* children of God. That is a familiar truth, so familiar that we do not realize its vast importance. It is a wonderful truth, an amazing truth. When I was a boy of eight, in 1864, the Prince of Wales, afterwards King Edward, visited this country, and the country went wild over him because he was the son of the Queen of England. But *we* are "the children of *God*," every believer in the Lord Jesus is a child of God, even the humblest, the poorest, the most ignorant believer in Jesus Christ. What

37

wonderful love it is that God has bestowed upon me that *I* should be *called* a child of God!

But it is not merely my privilege to be called so, I am so. This fact is not emphasized in the Authorized Version, but it is in the original, and therefore it is also in the Revised Version by the insertion of the clause that the Authorized Version omits, *"and such we are."*

Please notice the force of the "now" in verse 2, "Beloved, *now* are we children of God." The emphasis in the Greek is upon the "now," and therefore the emphasis should be upon the "now" in our rendering in the English. The thought is not that we are merely going to be children of God in some great and glorious day in the future, when we have been delivered of every last vestige of sin and imperfection, but that we *are so* now, at this very moment. No matter how weak you may be, no matter how many times you may have stumbled, no matter how little opportunity you may have had of studying the Word of God, and consequently how ignorant you may be, if you are really a believer in Jesus Christ you are already, at this very moment, a child of God. How our hearts should swell with holy pride and glory! I look at myself and see how poor a Christian I am and I am cast down, but I look at God's Word and I see there His sure declaration that I am a child of God after all, and I lift up my head, and my heart beats fast and strong and I cry, "I am a child of God. *Even I* am a child of God."

II. BELIEVERS SHALL BE LIKE JESUS WHEN HE COMES

The second great fact about believers in Jesus Christ is also found in the second verse, the last part of the verse: "We know, if he shall be manifested, *we shall be like him*; for we shall see

him even as he is." The second fact about believers here declared is that *when Jesus comes again we shall be like Him.*
That is not only a great fact, it is a glorious fact. To think that
there is a day coming, and perhaps coming very soon, when you
and I shall be just like the Lord Jesus. A good many of us are
not much like Him yet, even though we are believers in Christ.
Many of us who are professing Christians and who are really
saved people are not much like Him today.

In all my acquaintance with many of the best men and
women who ever lived on this earth I have never yet found
anyone who was as much like Jesus as I could wish. There is a
man whom I often speak of as being the most Christlike man
I ever knew, but even when I look at him and then look at
Jesus there is a wide gap between the two. There was a wide
gap between even Paul and Jesus. But the time is coming when
the poorest and weakest child of God here will be just like Jesus;
every beauty and every excellence and every glory of His character will be reproduced in you and me.

I sometimes think that these are the sweetest words in this
most wonderful of all books, the Bible, "We shall be like him;
for we shall see him even as he is." Sometimes when I work
hard to help a weak Christian and train him into what he ought
to be, and make poor headway and I am tempted to get discouraged, then this thought comes to me with great comfort,
"Well, the day is coming when all this failure will be over,
when he will be just like Jesus."

There is one man who always comes to my mind when I
reflect upon this verse. He was a man whom it was my privilege
to lead to Christ when he was perhaps 50 years of age. He
belonged to a good family, was well educated, had an excellent
mind, but had gone down through sin. He might have had a

good position in life, but he was working, when he worked at all, in the lumber camps in Minnesota. He came to me the first night I ever saw him, at the close of the service and took me aside and whispered tremblingly in my ear, "Do you think Jesus Christ could save me?" I replied, "I know He can, He can save anybody." Physically he was a big, stalwart, and a fine looking man in spite of the moral depths to which he had sunk. It was my privilege that night to lead him to Christ, and for a while he ran well, then he got discouraged and got to drinking, and for years his life was one perpetual up and down. He followed me from city to city, coming to me especially when he had fallen and was under the influence of liquor.

Sometimes I lost sight of him for months, but I never gave him up. I felt that the root of the matter was in him, and oftentimes when I was tempted to be discouraged and throw him overboard, the passage we are now studying would come to my mind, "When he shall appear we shall be like him," and I would say to myself, "When the Lord comes and Richard Campbell gets one look at Jesus Christ as He really is he will be so transformed into His perfect likeness that you can hardly tell the two apart."

Now notice when it is that we shall be like Him, when He comes, "When he is manifested," that is, when He is *made visible,* appears again in visible, bodily form. The Revised Version translates, *"If* He shall be manifested." This is a correct translation, but it is misleading to the ordinary English reader, for it implies a doubt that He is to be manifested, but according to the Greek idiom there is no doubt expressed in the Greek. John had no doubt on this point; he simply used a form of expression that emphasizes the fact that our becoming like Him *is conditioned upon* His coming. I shall not be like Him *until He comes.*

There are many people in these days who wonder why it is that some of us are longing for the Second Coming of Christ. This verse tells us one great reason why we are longing for the coming of Christ, because all our hope depends upon His coming again. It is when He comes that we shall be like Him. Don't you wish He would come today? I do.

And why is it we shall be like Him when He comes? Because "we shall see Him even as He is." It is beholding the Lord Jesus that makes us like Jesus even in the life that now is; it is through beholding Jesus that we become like Jesus. As Paul puts it in II Corinthians 3:18, English revision, "We all, with unveiled face reflecting as a mirror the glory of the Lord, are transformed into the same image from glory to glory, even as from the Lord the Spirit." As we look at Him day by day as He is revealed to us in the Word, we become more and more like Him, but now we see Him, as Paul tells us in I Corinthians 13:12, "in a mirror darkly," "but then [we shall see Him] face to face," see Him exactly as He is, and through seeing Him exactly as He is, be transformed into His own exact likeness.

III. THE BELIEVER DOES NOT MAKE A PRACTICE OF SIN

The third great fact about the believer in Christ we find in verses 5, 6, 9 and 10: "And ye know that he was manifested to take away sins; and in him is no sin. (6) Whosoever abideth in him sinneth not: whosoever sinneth hath not seen him, neither knoweth him. . . . (9) Whosoever is begotten of God doeth no sin, because his seed abideth in him: and he cannot sin, because he is begotten of God; (10) in this the children of God are manifest, and the children of the devil: whosoever doeth not righteousness is not of God, neither he that loveth not his brother." Here we see recorded this great fact about believers, that *true believers in Christ, those who have been born again, and are therefore abiding in Christ, do not make a practice of sin.*

These verses greatly puzzle many Christians, and make them question whether they are indeed the children of God. Verse 9 has been especially puzzling. It has puzzled more Christians than almost any other verse in the Bible. This verse declares, "Whosoever is begotten of God, doth not commit sin," or, as the Revised Version puts it, "Whosoever is begotten of God doeth no sin." And until one looks carefully at the verse it seems to teach that anyone born of God never commits a sin, so the puzzled reader says, "I sin quite often, and therefore I cannot be a child of God." What is the explanation? The explanation lies where the explanation usually lies in difficult passages of Scripture, that is, in noticing exactly what is said and noticing carefully the connection in which it is said. The first part of the explanation is found in the connotation, in John's own definition of sin. John has carefully defined what he means by sin five verses above, in verse 4: "Every one that doeth sin doeth also lawlessness: and *sin is lawlessness,*" or, as the Authorized Version puts it, "Sin is the transgression of the law." By "sin" therefore John means "transgression of the law," "lawlessness," that is such acts as reveal contempt for God's law as revealed in the Bible, conscious and intentional violation of the will of God as revealed in His Word. We may do many things which are not according to the will of God and yet they are not "sin" *in the sense in which John uses that word in this chapter.* They were violations of God's law, but they were not *conscious* and *intentional* violations of the law of God. They are sin in a very true sense, they certainly are sin according to a familiar definition of sin, "a lack of conformity to the will of God." And after the thing is done we will see that they are contrary to the law of God, and likely will see that we ought to have known that they were contrary to the law of God at the time of doing them, and will therefore confess them most humbly as "sin," but we did not see it at the time of doing it and it was not "sin" *in the sense that John carefully defines his use of the word "sin" here.*

The second part of the explanation is found in the tense of the verb used in verse 9. It is the present tense, and the exact force of the present tense, a force very frequently given it in the New Testament, is that it denotes *continuous* action. A literal translation of the verse would be, "Whosoever has been begotten out of God sin *is not doing,"* i.e., he is *not making a practice* of sin. John does not say that he never sins, but that he is not continuously doing sin, is not making a practice of sin. The translation of the Revised Version is more inaccurate than that of the Authorized Version. There is no warrant whatever in the Greek for the translation of the Revised Version, *"doeth no* sin." This translation of the Revised Version is not literal and does not give the sense. So what the verse says is that no one who has been born of God will go on doing things that he knows to be contrary to God's will.

If any of you are going on day after day consciously disobeying God you will do well to ask, "Am I really a child of God?"; and if you conclude that you are not, then you can become one today. But a person may be a child of God and still do things which are contrary to God's will, but not do them consciously and intentionally as known violations of God's will; and he may even do something which at the time of doing it he knows to be contrary to God's will, but he will not make a continuous practice of so acting. It is the believer's privilege to live without sinning. In the first verse of the preceding chapter John tells those to whom he writes, i.e., believers in Christ, that he writes these things for the purpose of keeping them from sinning. We can live every year and every day and every hour without doing that which at the time of doing it we know to be contrary to God's will; but if we study God's Word and are much in prayer, our view of God's will will constantly enlarge and things that we did today we cannot do tomorrow, and there will be abundant room for confession of our failure and *sin*.

IV. THE BELIEVER KNOWS THAT HE HAS PASSED OUT OF DEATH INTO LIFE

The fourth great fact about believers declared in this chapter we find in verse 14, "We know that we have passed out of death into life, because we love the brethren. He that loveth not abideth in death." The great fact here set forth about *the believer in Jesus Christ* is that he *has passed out of death into life, and knows it, too.* Every believer in Christ has "passed out of death into life." This our Lord Jesus Himself declares in John 5:24, "Verily, verily, I say unto you, he that heareth my word, and believeth him that sent me, hath everlasting life, and cometh not into judgment, but hath passed out of death into life." And again we read in John 3:36, "He that believeth on the Son hath everlasting life." It is every believer's privilege to know that he has everlasting life. Indeed John tells us in the fifth chapter and thirteenth verse of his book that he wrote this entire book for the express purpose that those who believe on the name of the Son of God might *know* that they *have eternal life.* It is doubtless true that there are those who believe on Jesus Christ who do not really know it, but it is their privilege to know it. But how do we know it? We know it by the testimony of God Himself, by God's testimony as found in His Word. God says so, and that settles it. God says the believer has eternal life in John 3:36 in the words already quoted, "He that believeth on the Son hath everlasting life." He says it again in John 5:24, and He says it elsewhere.

But that is not the way of knowing that we have eternal life of which John speaks in this verse. In this verse he says, "We know that we have passed out of death into life, *because* we love the brethren." Real faith in Jesus Christ leads inevitably to love for the brethren, and by the possession of this love of the brethren which springs up in our heart out of our faith in Jesus Christ "we know that we have passed out of death into life." Love is life. Hate and selfishness are death. If love has taken in my heart the place of hatred and selfishness, then I know I have passed out of death into life. But let me put to you a question. Do you really love the brethren? Do not answer the question too hastily. The tests of love given in this chapter in this immediate connection are very practical tests. We find them in verses 16 and 17, "Hereby know we love, because he laid down his life for us: and we ought to lay down our lives for the brethren: (17) but whoso hath the world's goods, and beholdeth his brother in need, and shutteth up his compassion from him, how doth the love of God abide in him?" If we lay down our life for the brethren, if we put our lives at their disposal (and, if necessary, actually sacrifice them, even as Jesus sacrificed His life) *then* we may know that we love the brethren, and therefore may "know that we have passed out of death into life." Our Lord Jesus Himself made love like this the test of discipleship. He says in John 13:34, 35, "A new commandment give I unto you, that ye love one another; even as I have loved you, that ye also love one another. (35) *By this* shall all men know that ye are my disciples, *if ye have love one to another.*"

The second test of love as set forth in these verses is a practical, everyday test. It is this, that if we have wherewith to supply another's need, that we actually do supply that other's need. Let me read it to you again for it is very searching: "Whoso hath the world's goods, and beholdeth his brother in need, and shutteth up his compassion from him, how doth the love of God abide in him?" You will please mark carefully that John does not say, "if I have enough for him and myself I divide." No, he says, "if I have enough for him, I use it for him, even if I have to go without myself." This certainly is very searching. How different God's tests of love from the tests that we often hear men giving. You will hear men as they stand up in prayer meeting talk something like this: "I know I have passed out of death into life because I love the brethren. I love to attend the prayer meeting and go where Christians go. I would rather go into a company of Christians than go to the best theater or opera or entertainment in the world." But that is no sure test that you love the brethren. Go at the close of the meeting to the same man who says this and tell him of a brother's need and see if he goes down into his pocket. That is the test that God gives, give what we have to meet the needs of others. That is the proof of love. "Is there such love?" someone asks. Yes, much of it. I would not have to go far to lay my hand on men who go without themselves that others may have.

And will you note carefully also who it is that the one who is born of God loves? He loves *"the brethren,"* i.e., any and all who are born of God. It does not make a particle of difference whether the brother be white or black or red, whether he be an American, or a Negro, or an Indian, or a Chinese, or a Japanese, or a Hindu, or a German or what he may be, *if he is a brother, one who is born of God, the one who "has passed out of death into life," loves him.* May I put to each one of you the question, and will you look it squarely in the face without flinching, "Do you love the brethren?" *If* you do you have "passed out of death into life."

V. The Believer Has Boldness Before God

The fifth great fact about believers in Jesus Christ is found in verses 19-21, "Hereby shall we know that we are of the truth, and shall assure our hearts before him: (20) because if our heart condemn us God is greater than our heart and knoweth all things. (21) Beloved, if our heart condemn us not, we have boldness toward God." *The believer has confidence, or boldness, before God.* The believer can go into God's presence and look up into His face and pour out his heart before Him, telling God everything that is in his heart. The word translated "confidence" in the Authorized Version, and "boldness" in the Revised Version, means literally, "all spokenness," it means fearless confidence, that frank and free open-heartedness in God's presence that pours its heart out unreservedly. It is our privilege to have this unreserved, frank, fearless confidence in our approach to God. This is indeed a wonderful privilege. It is indescribably blessed and glorious. Even the seraphim must veil their faces and their feet in His presence: but not so the believer in Jesus Christ. We can look up into His face with our faces unveiled and our hearts unafraid and tell Him all, just as a trustful child tells a true father. How reserved and trembling and hesitating we all are before great men, but it is our privilege to come right into the presence of the infinite God, the all holy God, with unhesitating, perfectly frank all-spokenness. This is indeed wonderful, it seems almost too wonderful to believe, but it is true, for God says it.

But when is it that we have this boldness toward God? Our verse answers the question, *when our hearts condemn us not*, especially when they condemn us not on this question of selfishness. If we know that we are selfish and our heart condemns us for our selfishness, or if there is some hidden or unconfessed sin in our hearts, we cannot have boldness before God; for we know that "He is greater than our heart, and knoweth all things." We know that even if the world does not know our sin He knows it. But when we are living the life of love, then we "assure our hearts before Him." If sin has been confessed, put away, if our hearts condemn us not, then we have this perfect, frank, fearless, childlike and trusting, unreserved confidence toward God.

VI. THE BELIEVER HAS POWER TO OBTAIN FROM GOD BY PRAYER WHATSOEVER HE ASKS

The sixth great fact regarding believers set forth in this chapter is found in verse 22, "And whatsoever we ask we receive of him, because we keep his commandments and do the things that are pleasing in his sight." The great fact here set forth is that *the believer has power to obtain from God by prayer whatsoever he asks*. That is not only a great fact, it is a tremendous fact, it is an amazing fact. Just to think of it, that it is your privilege and my privilege, if we are believers in Christ, to go to the infinite treasuries of God and help ourselves by prayer to whatever we desire. But perhaps someone says, "That is not my experience." Well, it is your privilege, and the verse tells you why it is not your experience. Let me read it again, "Whatsoever we ask we receive of him, *because we keep his commandments* and *do the things that are pleasing in his sight.*"

You see when it is we obtain whatsoever we ask, viz., when we keep God's commandments and do the things that are pleasing in His sight. In other words, if God is to listen to us we must first listen to Him. He has an open ear to our prayers when we have an open ear to His commandments. Are you making it your most earnest study to find out what the will of God is, and when you find it out to do it every time? Ah, there is the explanation why verse 22 is not your experience. But it is not enough that we keep His express commandments, we must also *"do the things that are pleasing in His sight."* There are many things that it would please God for you and me to do that He has not explicitly commanded us to do. God deals with us as a wise father deals with his child. I do not lay a law upon my children about everything I would like them to do, I leave them liberty, but I am rejoiced when in their liberty they make it their study to know what I would like, and when they do what they know would please me without waiting to be commanded. Just so it is with God. It pleases Him when we study to know His will about things which He has *not specifically commanded*, and when we do all that we think would please Him whether He has commanded it or not. When we make it the joyous study of our lives to please Him in everything, He makes it the joyous occupation of His life to bless us and answer all our prayers.

Here again we find the explanation of why verse 22 is not your experience. Honestly now before God, do you study in all things to know what would please God, and whenever you find what would please God do you do it *every time?* Ah, there are so many who call themselves Christians who are satisfied with doing just what is explicitly commanded. If you go to them with a higher duty, some duty the performance of which would bring new richness and fulness of blessing into their lives, they say, "Can you show me any place in the Bible where that is explicitly and plainly commanded?" Ah, that is not the question, the question is not is it plainly and explicitly commanded, but *would it please God?* You can apply this to theater-going, dancing, card playing, smoking, going to the movies, and a thousand and one other questions. Ah, some of you are on a very low plane of Christian living, and a plane where prayer has little power. Come up higher, come up where you study to know what would please God and where when one finds one more thing, little or great, that would please God, he does it with alacrity. Jesus Christ did always "the thing that pleased God" (John 8:29) and therefore Jesus could say to God, "I know that thou hearest me always" (John 11:42).

VII. BELIEVERS IN JESUS CHRIST HAVE THE GIFT OF THE HOLY SPIRIT

The seventh and final great fact about believers declared in this chapter is found in verse 24, "Hereby we know that he abideth in us, by the Spirit which he gave us." *The seventh great fact about believers* here set forth *is that, believers in Jesus*

*Christ have the Spirit given to them as a definite conscious ex-
perience,* i.e., they have the gift of the Holy Spirit. The gift of
the Spirit and the baptism with the Holy Spirit are practically
one and the same thing, as is perfectly plain from a comparison
of Acts 10:45 with Acts 11:15, 16. There are those who say
that the baptism with the Holy Spirit is not an individual experience but a corporate experience, i.e., the baptism with the
Holy Spirit is not given to the individual but given to the Church
as a body, but I notice that those who say this never give any
explicit Scripture to prove it. They expect us to accept this
statement upon their bare assertions. But to the Word and to
the testimony, what does the Book say? "Hereby we know that
he abideth in us, by the Spirit which he gave us." Here it is evident that a man knows when the Spirit is given to him, and
by knowing that, knows also that Christ abides, in him. Along
the same line turn to Matthew 3:11, where John the Baptist
says, "I indeed baptize you in water unto repentance: but he
that cometh after me is mightier than I, whose shoes I am not
worthy to bear: he shall baptize you in the Holy Spirit and in
fire." Now did John baptize, individually or corporately? Certainly individually. In the same way Jesus, if language means
anything, baptizes the individual believer with the Holy Spirit.
Turn again to Acts 1:5, "For John truly baptized with water,
but ye shall be baptized with the Holy Ghost, not many days
hence." Now compare Acts 2:1-4, where this promise was fulfilled. What does it say? "And it sat *upon each one* of them."
If the Word of God makes anything plain as day, it is that the
baptism with the Spirit is an individual experience, for each
individual believer in the Lord Jesus. Let us throw away then
the traditions of men and their ingenious theories and remote in-

ferences, and go by the plain, explicit teachings of the Word of God. To come back to our verse, the believer in Jesus has the gift of the Holy Spirit as an individual, conscious experience. But someone says, "That is not my experience." Perhaps not, verse 22 is not the experience of some believers, verse 14 is not the experience of some believers, and we saw why not. Can we see why not here? Yes, read the first part of the verse, "And *he that keepeth his commandments* abideth in him, and he in him." It is the believer who keepeth God's commandments who has the Holy Spirit given to him. Lack of obedience, lack of absolute surrender, is shutting many a professed believer in Jesus Christ out of the experimental possession of the Holy Spirit, but nevertheless the Holy Spirit is for them.

Many have heard Dr. Chapman tell the story of how he had been in the ministry for years and in many ways had been a successful minister, but through hearing Mr. Moody and reading Dr. F. B. Meyer he had been led to see that he did not have the fulness of the Holy Spirit, and one day he went alone in his study. From what Dr. Meyer had said he saw that in order to have the Holy Spirit he must make a complete surrender to God. He found he was unwilling to do it. He knelt down and asked God to make him willing to be willing, and God heard his prayer, and the will was surrendered, and he received the Holy Spirit, and his ministry was transformed. Some lack the Holy Spirit in their experience through lack of definite teaching along this line, some through lack of definite prayer (Luke 11:13; Acts 8:15, 16), but, nonetheless, the Holy Spirit is the blood-bought birthright of every believer in Jesus Christ. Jesus Christ at His ascension received the Holy Spirit for the whole Church, but alas, many do not claim their birthright.

My brother, claim your portion. Do not try to bring the Bible down to the level of your experience, bring your experience up to the level of the Bible, and this year will be by far the most happy and most fruitful year of your life.

Here then are seven great facts about the believer in Jesus Christ. The believer in Jesus Christ is *now*, already, today, a child of God.

I JOHN 4

Seven Great Lessons About Love

Introduction: In our study of the first chapter, we found *seven present and priceless privileges and possessions of the believer in Jesus Christ.* In the second chapter, *seven comforting views of Jesus,* in the third chapter, *seven great facts about believers in Jesus Christ,* and in this chapter we find *seven great lessons about love.* Before we take up these seven great lessons about love, let us notice an introductory note of warning with which John opens the chapter: "Beloved, believe not every spirit, but prove the spirits, whether they are of God. Because many false prophets are gone out into the world." There never was a time in which this warning was more needed than today. In this day in which we live, there is a great craving after communication with the spirit world, and a great longing for spirit control. Many are willing to listen to any spirit, and to any man who claims to be a prophet or teacher who gets his information directly from the unseen world. I am constantly receiving letters from men and women who claim to be inspired, and they may be inspired, but the question always arises in my mind, whether they are inspired of heaven or of hell. They may be spirit-controlled, but I wish to know before listening to them, what is the character of the spirit who controls them?

Men come to me and say, "I went to such and such a place, and heard a communication from the spirit world," and they fancy that any communication from the spirit world is worthy of attention and of faith. God here solemnly warns us against this very great folly. He says in the most explicit language, "Believe not every spirit, but *prove* the spirits, *whether they are of God*, for *many false prophets* are gone out into the world." So when a man or woman tells me that they have had a communication from the spirit world, I ask, "What spirit was it that spoke?" "Was it the Spirit of God or the spirit of Satan?" "Was it a true spirit or a false spirit?" Never forget for one moment that there are lying spirits as well as lying men; so prove the spirits, whether they are of God, and prove the prophets whether they are of God, whether they be true prophets or false prophets, whether they be prophets through which the Spirit of God speaks, or prophets through which the spirit of Satan speaks. You may set it down as certain that any spirit you have to go into a dark room to hear, and turn down all the lights, and who will only speak to you through some coarse woman or man of low mentality and doubtful morality and only speak for a money consideration of from $.50 to $50, I say that you may set it down for a certainty that any such spirit is a lying spirit, a dirty spirit.

There are false prophets too. God says in this verse that there are "many" of them. There have always been false prophets in the world, men of large pretensions and small spirituality, wolves in sheep's clothing, men who pretend to speak from God, but who only seek money and honor for themselves. There has never been a time in modern history when men and women who claim to be spirit-controlled were as numerous as they are today. Of course, much of this pretension to spirit control and spirit communication is cunningly concealed fraud, but it will not do to say that it is all pure fraud. There is such a thing as spirit control, control by demons, and God has forewarned us that in the last times there will be special developments along the line of spirit control. We read in I Timothy 4:1, "But the Spirit saith expressly, that in later times some shall fall away from the faith, *giving heed to seducing spirits* and *doctrines of demons,*" that is, doctrines taught by demons. We see this fulfilled in modern spiritualism, or as its devotees nowadays prefer to call it, occultism; we see it fulfilled in theosophy, we see it fulfilled also in some phases of the modern "tongues movement." Many of the developments in so-called "pentecostal gatherings" bear a most marked resemblance to the demonstrations that have been common in spiritualistic seances for years. Much of it is doubtless due to hysteria, but some of it is clearly due to evil spirits, demons, taking possession of well-meaning men and women who are so anxious for spirit-control that they do not stop to inquire about what spirit it is to whose control they are subjecting themselves. They forget the solemn warning of God in the first verse of this chapter, "Beloved, believe not every spirit, but prove the spirits, whether they are of God: because many false prophets are gone out into the world."

The important question arises: How can we know a false from a true spirit? John gives us in verses two and three an infallible test. "Hereby know ye the Spirit of God: every spirit that confesses that Jesus Christ is come in the flesh is of God: and every spirit which confesses not Jesus is not of God: and this is the spirit of anti-christ, whereof ye have heard that it cometh: and now is it in the world already." Here we note two things:

(1) First, the Spirit of God is constantly speaking of Jesus. *If a spirit is not speaking much of Jesus Christ, that spirit is not of God* (John 15:26). Indeed, if the spirit under whose influence one claims to be leads one to speak more of himself and

his personal experiences, or even more of the Holy Spirit, than he does of Jesus Christ, then that spirit is not of God.

(2) The second thing that we note by which we can tell the Spirit of God from false spirits, is that *the Spirit of God not merely witnesses of Jesus Christ, He witnesses of a Christ who became incarnate*. The Spirit of God not merely confesses Jesus Christ, but confesses Jesus Christ *"come in the flesh."* If any unseen power or person speaks to you, put to it the question, "Do you believe that Jesus Christ *came in the flesh?*" "Do you believe that God actually became incarnate in the person of Jesus of Nazareth?" If anyone comes to you claiming to be a prophet inspired of the Holy Spirit, put to him the question, "Do you believe that Jesus Christ 'came in the flesh'; do you believe that God actually became incarnate in the person of Jesus of Nazareth?" Unitarianism falls before that test; Christian Science falls down absolutely before that test. The fundamental postulate of Christian Science is that there is no such thing as flesh, that the body or flesh is "illusion," that it is "mortal thought" and "has no real existence." These words of John expose the utter falsity of Christian Science and its claims. John has anticipated, or rather *the Holy Spirit through John, has anticipated in this passage the whole colossal error of Christian Science.* A man may teach the truth about the incarnation of God in the person of Jesus of Nazareth, and be wrong on other points, though he is not likely to be; but *no lying spirit* will confess "Jesus Christ come in the flesh." The doctrine of the incarnation is the doctrine above all others that Satan and his hosts hate.

But suppose a spirit does not confess Jesus Christ "come in the flesh," suppose one who claims to be a prophet or teacher does not confess Jesus Christ "come in the flesh," what then?

The third verse answers the question, "every spirit which confesseth not Jesus is not of God: and this is the spirit of the
antichrist." Any spirit and any teacher that does not confess
Jesus of Nazareth as the actual incarnation of God is not of
God, and is "the spirit of Antichrist." Tried by this God-given
test, Unitarianism is not of God, it is of antichrist. Tried by
this test Christian Science is not of God, it is the spirit of antichrist.

While Christian Science talks much about Christ, it does
not mean *Jesus* Christ, the Christ "come in the flesh" in the
literal, historical person Jesus of Nazareth of the four gospels,
it means "the Christ principle." Christian Science does not even
admit the personality of God the Father, it believes not in a
personal God, it teaches that God is a principle. It says "God is
love and love is God."

But what safety is there for any of us if there are so many
false spirits and false prophets abroad? The fourth verse answers the question: "Ye are of God, my little children, and have
overcome them; because greater is he that is in you than he
that is in the world." The answer to put it in other words is,
if one is born of God, he is secure, and only when one is born
of God is he secure. This leads us naturally to the *seven great
facts about love* which the chapter teaches.

I. Love Is of God

You will find the first great lesson about love in *verse* 7,
"Beloved, let us love one another: for love is of [out of] God:
and every one that loveth is born of God and knoweth God."
This then is the first great lesson about love, that it is "of God,"
that is, it is of divine origin, begotten of God. Men say, "I
would like to see something that is divine." Well, look at love,

love is "of God," it is *out of* God, it had its origin in Him. Every particle of real love that there is in the world came from God. There is much in the world that we call love that is really not love, but is as far from love as darkness is from light. For example, you often see a man who says he loves a woman, but in reality he does not love the woman, he simply lusts after the woman and craves her for himself. Sometimes a man says he loves a woman and then shoots her because she will not marry him. Nothing could be further from love than that. Real love is not a desire to get others for ourselves; real love is a desire for, and a delight in the welfare of others, and when you find real love, you have found a divine thing. Love is the divinest thing in all the universe. Here is a man who has wisdom, here is another who has power, here is another who has love; this last man is the God-like man. Our wisdom will decay, our power will vanish, our love, if we have any, will abide eternally. "Now abideth faith, hope, love, these three; but the greatest of these is love" (I Corinthians 13:13).

Since love is of God, everyone that truly loves is born of God. This is what was given in our study of the preceding chapter as the test of the new birth. John there says, "We know that we have passed from death unto life, *because we love* the brethren. He that loveth not his brother abideth in death" (I John 3:14).

Do you love? "O yes," you say, "I love. I love my father, my mother, my children." Is that all? then you do not love, that is simply natural affection, which is a refined form of selfishness. Do you really love? What is the test whether you really love or not? The sixteenth and seventeenth verses of the preceding chapter answer the question. "Hereby perceive we the love of God, because he laid down his life for us: and we ought

to lay down our lives for the brethren. But whoso hath this
world's good, and seeth his brother have need, and shutteth
up his bowels of compassion from him, how dwelleth the love
of God in him?" The test and proof of love is that we are ready
to lay down our life for others, and that in the practical affairs
of everyday life when we see a brother in need, we are ready to
go down into our own pocket and give what we have in order
to meet his need.

II. GOD IS LOVE

The second great lesson about love we find in the next
verse, *verse 8* and also in *verse 16,* "He that loveth not knoweth
not God; for God is love," and "And we know and have believed the love that God hath in us. God is love: and he that
abideth in love abideth in God, and God abideth in him." So the
second great lesson taught here about love is that "God is love."
Not only is love *"of* God," but God Himself *is* love. Love is
the very essence of God's character. In chapter 1:5 we are told
that "God is light and in him is no darkness at all." Light is
love and love is light. That comes out in the second chapter,
the ninth to the eleventh verses: "He that saith he is in the light,
and hateth his brother, is in darkness even until now. He that
loveth his brother abideth in the light, and there is none occa-
sion of stumbling in him. But he that hateth his brother is in
darkness, and walketh in darkness, and knoweth not whither
he goeth, because that darkness hath blinded his eyes." *God is
love.* That is the great central truth around which the whole
system of Bible truth revolves. That is the great foundation
truth upon which the whole superstructure of Christian doctrine is built.

We owe our knowledge of this truth entirely to the Bible.
Take away the Bible and the facts therein recorded and thus

made known, and we have no conclusive proof that God is love. Therefore the people who accept the Bible doctrine that God is love, and then go to drawing inferences from that fact that contradict other plain declarations of the Bible, are most unreasonable and illogical. You must either accept the Bible or reject it. You cannot accept it in one breath and reject it in the next. If you do you are an intellectual trickster, a wretched pettifoger, and not an honest seeker after truth. If you reject the Bible you have no doctrine that God is love left upon which to build your universalist inferences. If you accept the Bible, you must also accept what it teaches about the eternal doom of those who reject Christ. Take whichever horn of the dilemma you please, and there is no room in either case for universalist hopes and fancies.

III. JESUS CHRIST IS THE SUPREME MANIFESTATION OF THE LOVE OF GOD

The third great lesson about love taught in this chapter we find in verses nine and ten, "Herein was the love of God manifested in us, that God hath sent his only begotten Son into the world, that we might live through him. Herein is love, not that we loved God, but that he loved us, and sent his Son to be the propitiation for our sins." The great lesson here taught about love is that *Jesus Christ is the supreme manifestation of the love of God.* "Herein was the love of God manifested in us, that God has sent His only begotten Son into the world, that we might live through Him" (verse 9). *God manifested His love, that is, showed it in a visible manner:*

1. *First of all, by sending His Son into the world.* That was wondrous condescension on God's part. This world was a rebellious world, an apostate world, but God sent His Son, His

only begotten Son, into it. "God so loved the world that He gave His only begotten Son, that whosoever believeth in Him should not perish, but have everlasting life" (John 3:16). That act of God filled Heaven with amazement. It ought to fill us with wonder, gratitude, praise and adoration. And why did God send His Son? "That we might live through Him." Without Christ we never could have lived. We would have "died in trespasses and sins." "The wages of sin is death," and we had done the work and earned the pay. Physical death, spiritual death, eternal death was our portion. But God would not have it so. He sent His Son that we might have life instead of death, "That we might live through Him." It is the same thought that the apostle Paul puts in another way in Romans 6:23, "For the wages of sin is death; but the [free] gift of God is eternal life in Christ Jesus our Lord." My friend, have you life or death today? You may have life. God sent His own Son, His only begotten Son into the world that you might have life through Him. Will you take this life through Him?

2. In the second place, *God manifested His love in Christ in a still further and more wonderful way,* as stated in verse ten. "Herein is love, not that we loved God, but that he loved us, and sent his Son to be the propitiation for our sins." That is to say, He not only sent His only begotten Son into the world, but *He sent Him to be the propitiation for our sins.* Propitiation means, "a means of appeasing," that is, a means of appeasing God's holy wrath at sin. We had sinned; God was holy; God's holy wrath at sin must fall upon us and destroy us unless a propitiation was provided; God provided it Himself, and that propitiation was nothing less than *His own Son dying a death of immeasurable agony and shame on the cross of Calvary for us.* "Christ died" (Galatians 3:13). Oh amazing love of God,

amazing God of love, to Himself provide at immeasurable cost to Himself for the security of those against whom His holy wrath blazed.

IV. If God So Loved Us We Ought Also to Love One Another

The fourth great lesson about love we find in *verse 11*, "Beloved, if God so loved us, we ought also to love one another." *The great lesson here taught about love is that, if God so loved us, we ought also to love one another.* That lesson needs little comment, but it needs much exemplification in our daily lives. How absurd our selfishness looks in the light of God's wondrous love. God loved me enough to give His Son to die for me, and I do not love my brother enough to make the smallest sacrifice for him. How awful the mad rush of men for their own gain, trampling down everyone who gets in their way, seems in the light of the wondrous love of God, and the tremendous sacrifice God made for us. How appalling and awful war looks in the light of God's wondrous love for us; yes, how appalling looks the scramble among the Allies for each one to get the most and sacrifice the least for the others. Oh, that these words might sink deep into our hearts and transform our lives, "Beloved, if God so loved us, we ought also to love one another."

V. He That Loveth Others Dwelleth in God and God in Him

The fifth great lesson about love we find in verses twelve to sixteen, "No man hath beheld God at any time: if we love one another, God abideth in us, and his love is perfected in us: hereby know we that we abide in him and he in us, because he hath given us of his Spirit. And we have beheld and bear witness that the Father hath sent the Son to be the Saviour of the world. Whosoever shall confess that Jesus is the Son of God, God abideth in him, and he in God: and we know and have believed the love which God hath in us: God is love, and he that abideth in love, abideth in God, and God abideth in him." *The great lesson here taught about love is that he that loveth another abideth (or dwelleth) in God and God in him.* What a wonderful thought it is that God should dwell in me. What a wonderful thought it is that I should dwell in God; but this is my standing and my state if I love others: I dwell in God, God dwells in me. Many are saying today, "I want to live in America, or I want to live in Southern California, or I want to live in this great country or beautiful place or that." Oh, there is a better dwelling place than Southern California, that is God. If I love, I dwell in God and God dwells in me. Love is indeed a wonderful thing, a glorious thing, a divine thing. To have it is infinitely better than to have all the wealth and honor and pleasure of earth. Do we really love? Do you love? Do I? Have you renounced self utterly, and do you rejoice in spending and being spent for others? Are you glad to sacrifice your welfare for the sake of the welfare of others? If so, God dwells in you, and you dwell in God. That is heaven on earth; a life of love, a life of sacrifice of self for the good of others, is heaven upon earth. God's statement that if we love we dwell in God and God in us would be enough, but we have something beside the mere statement; we have the conscious possession of the Spirit. "Hereby know we," says John, "that we dwell in Him and He in us, because He hath given us of His Spirit." The one who loves has the Holy Spirit and knows that he has the Holy Spirit. Many are wondering why they do not receive the Holy Spirit. Do you not find the answer here? Do you really love? Have you renounced self and its interests entirely and given yourself up to live for the glory of God and the good of your fellow men? If not, do it today.

But the great secret of loving others is being born of God. "Everyone that loveth is begotten of God." Let us receive Jesus that we may be born of God, (John 1:12). Then we shall love, and then we shall receive the Holy Ghost. But if you have not received the Holy Spirit, don't try to comfort yourself by saying that "the baptism with the Holy Spirit is a corporate and not an individual experience." It is not so. The baptism with the Holy Spirit is an individual experience. Claim it, and if you do not receive it, ask yourself, have you met the condition, do you really love?

VI. THERE IS NO FEAR IN LOVE

The sixth great lesson about love we find in *verse 18,* "There is no fear in love: but perfect love casteth out fear, because fear hath punishment: and he that feareth is not made perfect in love." The great lesson about love taught here is, that *"there is no fear in love, but perfect love casteth out fear."* Learn to love God, and you will be delivered from all dread of God. You will still reverence God, but you will not be afraid of God. You will have such a holy awe of Him as you never had before, but there will be no dread in that awe, but child-like trust. There will be no shrinking away from God, but rather a cuddling up to Him as a child to its mother's bosom. "Perfect love casteth out fear." What wonderful words! The only way to get freed from the fear of God is to learn to love Him.

I can remember the days when I was afraid of God. I did not like to think of God, and yet I was afraid not to think of Him. That is all past now. I would rather think of God than to think of anyone else or anything else. That is one great reason why I love the Bible, because it tells me about God. The reason why I love it more than all other books put together is because it tells me more about God than all other books put together. I have no fear of God, I absolutely trust Him. I sink down into His everlasting arms, and there is where I rest. "There is no fear in love, for perfect love casteth out fear." Do you fear God? Are you afraid of God? If you are, you are not yet made perfect in love. But someone asks, "How can I learn to love God with that perfect love that casteth out fear?" The next division of our exposition will tell us this.

VII. WE LOVE BECAUSE HE FIRST LOVED US

The seventh great lesson about love we find in *verse 19,* "We love, because he first loved us." *The great lesson here taught us about love is, that we love because God first loved us.* Love does not begin with our loving God, but with God loving us. There are those who say, especially to children, "You love God, and God will love you." That is entirely false teaching, it is getting the cart before the horse. Love begins with God loving us. He loved us while we still hated Him, or as Paul puts it in Romans 5:8, "God commendeth his love toward us in that while we were yet sinners, Christ died for us." When His love to us causes us to love Him, then He pours out upon us a still larger measure and better quality of love. As our Lord Jesus puts it in John 14:21-23, "He that hath my commandments and keepeth them, he it is that loveth me, and he that loveth me shall be loved of my Father, and I will love him and will manifest myself unto him. If a man love me he will keep my words: and my Father will love him, and we will come unto him and make our abode with him."

But it all begins by God loving us. When we know and believe the love that God has to us, then we will begin to love God.

How many a man has learned to love God by meditating on John 3:16! I knew a hardened and desperate criminal whose hard heart was broken by just hearing Romans 5:8, "God commendeth His love toward us in that while we were yet sinners, Christ died for us." Mrs. J. K. Barney tells the story of a dying miner, utterly hardened and unapproachable, whose heart was broken and life transformed by telling him of the Man who died for him.

1. If you do not love God, do not try to pump up love for Him, simply meditate on His love for you. A little girl once came to Mark Guy Pearse, the great English preacher, and said, "Oh, Mr. Pearse, I don't love God; I wish I did love God." The great preacher replied, "Little girl, you go home today and keep saying over and over to yourself, 'God loves me, God loves me, God loves me,' and I think you will come next Sunday saying, 'I love God.'" The following Sunday the little girl rushed up to the great preacher with a face full of sunshine, and said, "Oh, Mr. Pearse, I do love God, I do love God. As I went away last Sunday I kept saying to myself, 'God loves me, God loves me,' and I began to think of His love, and I saw Jesus hanging on the cross for my sin, and my cold heart began to get warm, and the first I knew my heart was full of love to God." Oh, it is the simplest thing in the world to love God, a child can understand it; just dwell upon the love of God to you, until your hard and selfish heart is broken, and you love God.

2. But God's love to us not only awakens in our hearts a love to God, but it begets love to man as well. This comes out in a striking way in the Revised Version. In the Authorized Version we have, "We love *Him* because he first loved us," but

the Revised Version leaves out *"Him"* and reads, "We love, because He first loved us." That is to say, God's love to us not only begets love to Him, but begets love to all. This is the way to learn to love men, even to love the unloveliest of men. Dwell on God's love to you, and dwell on your unworthiness of that great love. Our great need today is love, love to fellow Christians, love to the vile and outcast, love to the most abandoned men and women, love to the heathen whom we never saw, love to the Chinese, love to the Africans. What this old world is dying for is love. The reason why governments and institutions are crumbling, the reason why not merely nations are rising against nations, but classes are rising against classes, and murdering one another is because of the lack of love. No peace leagues that man can devise will set things straight, nothing but love begotten in the hearts of men by the power of the Holy Ghost. "Whence come wars, and whence come fightings among you? come they not hence, even of your pleasures that war in your members?" asks God in James 4:1. Man's answer is "Wars arise because of imperfect forms of government, because of a lack of real democracies." Man's answer is nonsense. Democracies have waged as bitter wars as autocracies ever did. God's answer is the true one, "Come they not hence? Even of your pleasures that war in your members?" Wars come, and all miseries come, from living for our own pleasure instead of living the life of love. If all men would only give Christ the reign in their hearts, to fill their hearts with love, all wars, wars between nations, wars between classes, would cease in a moment.

How shall we get this love that will be the solution of all our difficulties in church and nation and between the nations? By dwelling on the love of God to us. "We love, because He first loved us." Meditate every day on God's love to you, and its many and wondrous manifestations to you. Think of that love when you kneel in prayer, think of it when you go to the Lord's Table, think of it as you read your Bible, think of it as you go to your work. Like begets like, and love begets love. "We love Him because He first loved us."

I JOHN 5

THE SEVEN-FOLD GLORY OF THE BELIEVER IN JESUS CHRIST

INTRODUCTION: In this chapter, the last in the book, we find set forth, *The Seven-Fold Glory of the Believer in Jesus Christ*.

I. THE BELIEVER'S NOBLE PARENTAGE

The first factor in the Seven-fold Glory of the Believer in Jesus Christ we find in the first verse: "Whosoever believeth that Jesus is the Christ is born [begotten] of God." Here we are shown *The Believer's Noble Parentage;* God is his Father; he is begotten of God. Every true believer in Jesus Christ can boast of the Eternal, All-wise, All-holy, Almighty God as his Father. We are so familiar with this truth that we lose sight of its wonderful meaning. If it were published in any of our papers that a son of the Queen of England were to visit the city, the whole city would be moved with excitement, they would wish to get a glimpse of this son and heir of one of Europe's kingdoms who still retains his throne. I remember when I was a boy of eight, Queen Victoria's son, the Prince of Wales, afterward King Edward, visited this country, and the whole country was filled with excitement. People went great distances and to great lengths just to get a look at this child of a queen. I was in Albion, Michigan, at my grandfather's home when he passed through there, and a colored boy who worked for my grandfather went down to the train, and with enterprising agility climbed up on the outside of the car and looked into the window where the Prince of

70

Wales sat. Others were as eager as he to get a look at him, but not so successful. The colored boy came back home in great disgust and said, "Why! he doesn't look any different from any other man."

Even in this day when all the thrones of earth seem to be tottering, most of us think it a great thing to be the child of a king, or a child of some great man of letters, or of some great scholar or of some man who has achieved greatness in other lines. But what is it to be the child of the greatest of earth's monarchs, or the greatest of millionaires or the greatest of statesmen, or the greatest of generals in comparison to being the child of the great King of Kings and Lord of Lords? And that is what each one of us who believes in Christ is, "Whosoever believeth that Jesus is the Christ is begotten of God." Of course, the faith that Jesus is the Christ that makes us children of God, must be a real faith, not a mere intellectual conviction that Jesus is the Messiah, God's anointed king, but a heart conviction that leads us to make Him our King, that leads us to enthrone Him as King in our heart, and leads us to confess Him as such before the world. Anyone of us, no matter how poor, or in what humble circumstances we may be, how ignorant we are, or even how vicious we have been in the past, who will today really put his faith in Jesus as the Christ, as his anointed King, to whom he surrenders absolutely the control of his life, that one becomes instantly *a child of God*. We find the same truth set forth by John in his gospel, the first chapter and the twelfth verse, "But as many as received Him, to them gave He the right to become the children of God, even to them that believe on His name." Is it not wonderful? As I look over a group of Christian people, what do I see? Merely a company of men and women of various ranks in life who sincerely believe in and are trying to serve the Lord Jesus? No, I am looking out upon a company of the truest noblemen and noblewomen in the universe, men and women who occupy a place above the angels, "children of God," one and all, provided you really believe that Jesus is the Christ.

But this noble position that each believer in Christ occupies, lays upon us a corresponding responsibility. First of all, that we live worthy of this high calling wherewith we are called, and second that we love every other believer in Jesus Christ, for every other believer is a child of God, and this same verse tells us that if we love God who begat us, we must necessarily love "him also that is begotten of Him," and every believer in Jesus Christ is thus begotten. I am under the most solemn obligation to love every believer in Jesus Christ, no matter to what nation he may belong, no matter what his color may be, no matter what his education or lack of education may be, no matter what his position in human society is, he is a child of God, and as I love Him that begat, I must also love him that is begotten of Him. This is very solemn, and it suggests a question that I must put to everyone. Do you love every believer in Jesus Christ? Whether he be English or French or Japanese or Korean or Chinese or German or African or whatever he may be? Pretty much everywhere my children go, they find men and women who take the deepest interest in them. Why? Because they are my children, and these people love me and therefore they love my children. If we love God, we love everyone of God's children.

But how do we know that "every one that believes Jesus is the Christ is begotten of God"? We know it because God says so, says so here, and God's Word is enough, we need no other proof.

II. The Believer's Splendid Victory

The second element in *the Seven-fold Glory of the Believer in Jesus Christ* we find in verses four and five, "For whatsoever is begotten of God overcometh the world: and this is the victory that hath overcome the world, even our faith. And who is he that overcometh the world, but he that believeth that Jesus is the Son of God?" We see here *The Believer's Splendid Victory*, victory over the world. We live in a day in which our papers are full of applause for those who have won victory on the field of battle. We are receiving back our brave soldiers who risked all and won, with cordial welcomes. Yesterday as our returning victors marched down the streets, the streets were filled with applauding multitudes, and well they might be. But great as were the victories that these soldiers won, they are really nothing to the victory that every child of God has every day of his life, victory over the world that hates God and all that belongs to God. There is no other victory so great and glorious as that. The world is at enmity with God, and the world is constantly exercising an influence over us, to drag us down from our loyalty to God into conformity to the world, and on every hand well-meaning men and women are being floored by the world. They are lowering their flag, they are sacrificing their high ideals, they cannot resist the pressure of the world and its allurements; but it is the privilege of every believer in Jesus Christ, everyone who truly believes from the heart that Jesus is the Son of God, to have victory over the world, every day and every hour and every moment. How is this victory won? Simply by faith in Jesus Christ. "This is the victory that overcometh the world, even our faith." Faith in Jesus Christ, faith that Jesus Christ is all He claims to be, the Christ, the Son of God, God manifest in the flesh, real faith that leads us to put away sin and surrender our lives absolutely to His control, brings victory.

The reigning philosophy of today says the way to get victory over the world is by "the power of the will." So, says God, "Who is he that overcometh the world?" Listen to God's answer, "He that believeth that Jesus is the Son of God." Do you believe that Jesus is the Son of God? That God dwelleth in all His fullness in Him, that in Jesus dwells all the fullness of the Godhead bodily? You say, "Yes I do," but do you really? You may be orthodox in your conception of the person of Jesus Christ, but do you really believe in your heart that Jesus is the Son of God? If you really do, you will show it by having victory over the world. The world may come to you with its most subtle and its most powerful allurements, but it will have no power over you, for you will believe that Jesus is the Son of God with a belief that leads you to surrender your whole life to that great truth. Whatever the world may promise to you or offer you it will have no allurement. The only question will be, "What does the Son of God bid me do?" And knowing that, in the strength that He gives you, you will do it, and you will have victory over the world.

III. THE BELIEVER'S PRICELESS POSSESSION

Now let us turn to the eleventh and twelfth verses, "And the witness is this, that God gave unto us eternal life, and this life is in his Son. He that hath the Son hath the life: he that hath not the Son of God hath not the life." Here we find *The Believer's Priceless Possession*, the believer has eternal life. Here is another wonderful phrase, "eternal life," but one with which we are so familiar that this, too, has lost much of its significance, unless we stop to ponder the full import of the words. When we do stop and weigh the meaning of the words, we see that this world has nothing to offer in comparison to what the Lord Jesus Christ gives to everyone who believes on Him — eternal life. What is eternal life? It is a life which is not merely endless in its duration, but infinite in its quality. It is the life of God Himself imparted to us. This is revealed in the opening verses of this epistle: "That which was from the beginning, that which we have heard, that which we have seen with our eyes, that which we beheld and our hands handled, concerning the Word of Life, (and the life was manifested, and we have seen, and bear witness, and declare unto you the life, the eternal life, which was with the Father, and was manifested unto us)." Here we are told that eternal life is the life which was manifested in the person of Jesus, and that that life which was manifested in the person of Jesus was the life which God the Father Himself had. So we say on the warrant of God's Word, that eternal life is not merely a life which is endless in its duration, but a life which is divine and infinite in its quality, the very life of God imparted to us and dwelling in us.

This eternal life is in Jesus Christ, and whoever takes Jesus Christ gets this life, or as John puts it in the twelfth verse, "He that hath the Son hath the life; and he that hath not the Son of God hath not the life." It is evident from this that life is more than mere existence, for many who have not the Son of God certainly have existence, but they haven't "life." But anyone who receives the Son of God, who takes Him to be to them what He offers Himself to be, that one instantly gets "eternal life." It is true that we get it in the beginning only in its germ, and that it will take all the endless ages of eternity for it to develop in its fullness, but eternal life is ours the moment we accept Jesus Christ. This same truth we find time and time again in the Bible; for example, we find it in John 3:36, "He that believeth on the Son *hath* everlasting life." Everyone that truly believes on Jesus Christ, even though he be a weak and faltering and stumbling Christian, nevertheless has eternal life. It is our privilege not only to have eternal life if we are believers in Christ, it is also our privilege to know that we have eternal life. This is pointed out in the next verse, the thirteenth, "These things have I written unto you, *that ye may know* that ye have eternal life, even unto you that believe on the name of the Son of God." John wrote this entire epistle for the specific purpose above all else, that men not only might have eternal life, but that they may know that they have eternal life. He wrote his gospel that men might obtain eternal life through believing on the Son of God whom he presented in that gospel. This he plainly declares in John 20:31, "These are written *that ye may believe* that Jesus is the Christ, the Son of God; *and that believing ye may have life* in his name." But he wrote his epistle that those who have eternal life through believing on Jesus Christ *might know* that they have eternal life. Time and time again when I have put to people the question, "Have you eternal life?" they have replied, "I hope so, but I do not think that any one can say that he *knows* that he has eternal life." But this verse distinctly says that we "may *know* that we have eternal life," that this epistle was written for the specific purpose that we might know that we have eternal life. It is the privilege of every believer in Jesus Christ to know that he has eternal life, not merely to think so, not merely to hope so, not merely to believe so, but to know it. Oh wonderful privilege! I would rather know that I had eternal life than to have the wealth of all the Rockefellers, and Morgans, and other millionaires of earth. Their wealth will soon all be gone, and they will be the poorest of the poor, but oh, to know that you have eternal life, the very life of God, and that this life will never end!

I shall never forget the night when it burst upon me in all the fullness of its meaning, that I really had eternal life. I had believed for a long time that I had eternal life, and indeed in a way I had assurance that I had eternal life, but I had never *realized* what it meant. It was one Sunday night; it had been a busy day; I think I had walked twelve miles that day, and I had preached many times. I was going home; I was on the last mile of the twelve, yes the last quarter mile; it was a beautiful moonlight night, and I saw my house in the distance. I was reflecting on some passage of Scripture, I think it was John 10:28, 29, "I give unto them eternal life; and they shall never perish, and no one shall snatch them out of my hand. My Father, who hath given them unto me, is greater than all; and no one is able to snatch them out of my Father's hand." My heart was opened not merely to believe these words but to realize them. I was alone on the street late at night, and I shouted, "I have eternal life, I have eternal life, I shall never perish," and my heart was almost overwhelmed with joy.

It is the privilege of the humblest child of God to have that same assurance and the same realization. The only basis that you need for that assurance is God's Word. You do not need some feeling, you do not need some testimony of the Holy Spirit, though you will have that too in time, if you will just take God at His Word. Here is God's own Word, and that is enough, *"He that hath the Son hath the life."* Have you the Son of God? Have you accepted Jesus Christ as your personal Saviour? Have you surrendered to Him as your Lord, and are you confessing Him as such before the world? Are you striving to live to please Him in everything day by day? Do you really believe on the Son of God? If you do, you have eternal life, you will never perish, no man nor devil will have power to snatch you out of the hand of the Father and the Son, you are as eternally safe today as you will be after you have been inside the pearly gates ten million years. Oh the glory of it! To have eternal life and to know that you have it.

IV. THE BELIEVER'S SURE CONFIDENCE

Now let us read the two following verses, verses fourteen and fifteen, "And this is the boldness, [confidence] which we have toward him, that, if we ask anything according to his will, he heareth us: and if we know that he heareth us whatsoever we ask, we know that we have the petitions which we have asked of him." Here we have *The Believer's Sure Confidence*. That confidence is of a wonderful sort. The confidence of the believer in Jesus Christ is that if we ask anything, no matter what it may be, that is according to His will, God hears us, and we know further that if He hears us whatsoever we ask, that we have the very thing that we have asked of Him, that the petition that we have asked is ours. Isn't that wonderful, to be able to go back to God and ask Him anything that we desire that is according to His will, and to know that He hears our prayer, and that anything according to His will is ours? We may not have the actual enjoyment of it for days or weeks or months, but God has granted it and it is ours, just as much ours as it will be afterwards when we shall actually see it in our hands. One day I asked God for $5000 that was greatly needed in our work in Chicago, and God gave me to see that what I asked was according to His will, and I knew that that for which I asked was mine, and arose from my knees with the glad consciousness that the $5000 was mine. I was in Northfield, Massachusetts, and the next day (if I remember correctly) word came to Mr. Fitt in Chicago from the Metropolitan Bank, that a bank at Indianapolis had telegraphed that a man in Indianapolis, of whom I had never heard, and who had never given us anything before, and as far as I know has never given us anything since, had placed $5000 in the bank there subject to our call. Then we actually had it in experimental possession, but it was really ours the night before when God heard my prayer. Oh, how wonderful to have access to the One who has infinite resources, "who is able to do exceeding abundantly above all that we ask or think," and to be able to ask Him for anything that we need, anything that is according to His will, and know that our prayer is heard, and our petition granted, and the thing asked for ours.

But can we know what is according to God's will? We certainly can. We can know it in two ways: First of all, we can know it by the promises in the Book. The Bible was given to us to reveal the will of God. The promises are especially given to us to show us what it is God's will to give us, and when we have any specific promise we can take it to God with the absolute assurance that the thing which we are asking is in accordance with His will, and that we will get the thing which we ask. But there are many things that we need, or think we need, that are not specifically promised in the Word of God. Can we know the will of God in such a case as that? Yes, Romans 8: 26, 27 tells us how, "In like manner the Spirit also helpeth our infirmity; for we know not how to pray as we ought; but the Spirit Himself maketh intercession for us with groanings which cannot be uttered; and He that searcheth the hearts knoweth what is the mind of the Spirit, because He maketh intercession for the saints according to the will of God." This tells us plainly that it is the work of the Holy Spirit to reveal God's will to us as we pray, and to lead us to pray for things according to His will. How often when I have been in prayer, when I did not know that the thing which I was asking was definitely promised in the Word, the Holy Spirit has made clear to me that it was according to the will of God, and I have asked for it with absolute confidence, and gotten it from Him.

V. THE BELIEVER'S WONDERFUL POWER

Now we come to something if possible even more wonderful, that is found in verse sixteen, "If any man see his brother sinning a sin not unto death, he shall ask, and he shall give him life for them that sin not unto death." Here we see *The Believer's Wonderful Power*. What is that power? Power to save by his prayer, his erring brother's life. He has power not only to secure salvation for himself, but to secure salvation and eternal life for a sinning brother. The death spoken of in this verse is eternal death, the life spoken of is eternal life. There are two words in the Greek New Testament for life. John uses one of these two words here, the one for spiritual life; John never uses this word for natural life. This verse is often taken to teach divine healing, but that is not the thought of the verse; the thought is, that we can secure life, spiritual life, eternal life for a sinning brother.

This is the wonderful power that God has put into our hands. It is a power that we ought to exercise more frequently than we do. Is it not wonderful to think that we can not only get life for ourselves, but life for others; life for those who are down in the depths of sin; life for anyone, no matter how grossly he has sinned, if he has not committed the one unpardonable sin? Oh, how many sinning ones there are around about us;

how much they need our prayers. Are we using this mighty instrument of prayer as much as we ought in securing life, life everlasting for others? There is illustration after illustration from my own experience and observation, how life has been obtained, eternal life, for apparently the most hopeless, by prayer.

VI. THE BELIEVER'S PERFECT SECURITY

Now let us look at verse eighteen: "We know that whosoever is begotten of God sinneth not: but he that was begotten of God keepeth him, and the evil one toucheth him not." Here we find *The Believer's Perfect Security*. There is a notable change in the Revised Version from the Authorized. The Authorized Version reads, "We know that whosoever is born of God sinneth not; but he that is begotten of God keepeth himself, and that wicked one toucheth him not." But the Revised Version reads, "We know that whosoever is begotten of God sinneth not but he that *was* begotten of God [that is, Jesus Christ] keepeth him [that is, keeps the one who is begotten of God], and the evil one toucheth him not." The American Revised Version, while it agrees with the English revision in much in this verse, goes back to the Authorized in translating the word after "keepeth," "himself" and not "him." It is a question of the original text, and the translation of the English Revision is to be preferred, and the thought is, that the only begotten Son of God, Jesus Christ, keeps from sinning everyone that is begotten of God so that the Evil One touches him not.

This is in accordance with what is so frequently taught elsewhere in the Bible, by Jesus Christ Himself, and by others, that it is Jesus who does the keeping and not we ourselves. As Jesus puts it in John 10:28, in a verse already quoted, "I give unto them eternal life, and they shall never perish, and no one shall *snatch them out of my hand.*" We find the same truth in Jude, 24 and 25, "Now unto Him that is able to guard you from stumbling and to set you before the presence of His glory without blemish in exceeding joy, to the only God our Saviour, through Jesus Christ our Lord, be glory, majesty, dominion, and power, before all time, and now and forevermore." It is the only begotten Son of God who does the keeping, and He is abundantly able to keep. He is able to keep us from sinning and from thus being lost. He is able to keep us every day and every hour so that we do not make a practice of that which we know to be contrary to the will of God. We cannot keep ourselves, but He can keep us. I have no fears that the devil will ever get me. I know that he is far wiser and far stronger than I am, but I also know that the only begotten Son of God who is my keeper, is far wiser and far stronger than he, and that though Satan is a "strong man armed," Jesus Christ is "stronger than he" and able to despoil him of his goods, and that He has delivered me from his power, and that He will keep me through His power forever.

I was testifying one night on the streets of Minneapolis to my security and my safety. Later on in the evening a man who had stood in the crowd came to me and said, "Mr. Torrey, you ought not to have such confidence in yourself, you may fall after all." I replied, "I have no confidence at all in myself. No one knows better than I how weak I am, but I have confidence in Jesus Christ, and He has covenanted to keep me from falling, He has said that He has given me eternal life, and that no one shall ever snatch me out of His hand." Jesus Christ keeps everyone who is begotten of God from the practice of sin and from the clutch of Satan.

VII. THE BELIEVER'S GLORIOUS KNOWLEDGE

Now we come to the last element in *The Seven-fold Glory of Believers in Jesus Christ*. You will find it in the twentieth verse, "And we know that the Son of God is come, and hath given us an understanding, that we know him that is true, and we are in him that is true, even in his Son Jesus Christ." Here we have *The Believer's Glorious Knowledge*. The Son of God gives to every believer in Him an understanding to know God. He gives to every believer a thorough comprehension of God. The knowledge of God is the supreme knowledge, the knowledge of God is infinite knowledge. We cannot by searching find out God. We can find out a little about Him through the study of nature. By the study of geology, astronomy, biology and other sciences we can see something of the marvelous wisdom and stupendous power of God. By the study of history, we can see something of the righteousness of God, we can see how throughout the whole history of man "one increasing purpose runs." We can read in history how God is a righteous God, and how nations as well as individuals in the final outcome reap just what they sow. We can see in all history how "there is a power not ourselves that makes for righteousness"; but the deeper depths of God's being we can never fathom from the study of science or history. We can only come to the real vital knowledge of God by the gift of God's Son, our Saviour; but He does give us through the Holy Spirit as John here declares, "an understanding that we may know God." The humblest and most illiterate of God's children, the humblest and most illiterate of believers in Jesus Christ has more real knowledge, knowledge that counts for time and eternity, the only knowledge that is really worth while, the knowledge of God, than the greatest savant, or scientist, or philosopher, or university professor, who does not believe in Jesus Christ. The great scientists and philosophers may study and study and study, and explore and explore and explore, but they will never come to know God if they lack the power of spiritual apprehension. Though open-eyed to the facts of nature, they are blind as a bat to the facts about God. But it is the humblest believer's privilege to have a thorough and living knowledge of God.

Conclusion

Here then we see the *Sevenfold Glory of the Believer in Jesus Christ.*

1. The Believer's Noble Parentage Begotten of God.

2. The Believer's Splendid Victory — victory over the world.

3. The Believer's Priceless Possession — Eternal Life.

4. The Believer's Sure Confidence, i.e., that if he ask anything according to the will of God he will obtain it.

5. The Believer's Wonderful Power — Power to obtain life, eternal life for sinning men and women.

6. The Believer's Perfect Security — Kept by the power of the only begotten Son of God from the practice of sin, and the clutch of Satan.

7. The Believer's Glorious Knowledge — thorough, comprehensive, vital knowledge of God.

Indeed, it pays to be a believer in Jesus Christ.